PUERTO RICO

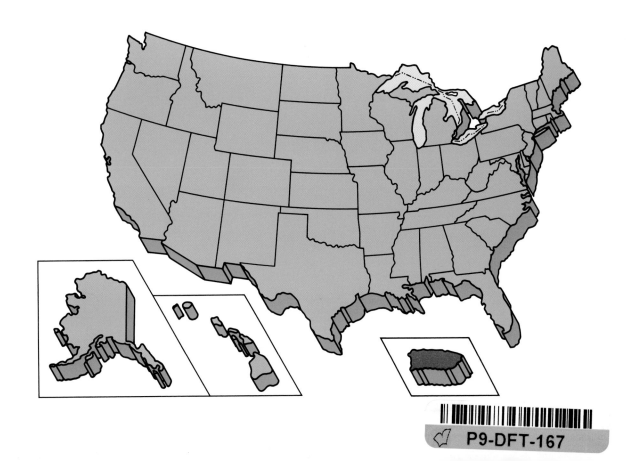

P9-DFT-167

Hello U.S.A.

PUERTO RICO

Joyce Johnston

Lerner Publications Company

Copyright © 1995 by Lerner Publications Company,
Minneapolis, Minnesota.

All rights reserved. International copyright secured. No part of this
book may be reproduced, stored in a retrieval system, or transmitted
in any form or by any means—electronic, mechanical, photocopying,
recording, or otherwise—without the prior written permission of Lerner
Publications Company, except for the inclusion of brief quotations in
an acknowledged review.

This book is available in hardcover, paperback, and Spanish-language editions
Library binding by Lerner Publications Company
Soft cover by First Avenue Editions
241 First Avenue North
Minneapolis, MN 55401
ISBN: 0-8225-2752-9 (English edition)
ISBN: 0-8225-2753-7 (Spanish edition)
ISBN: 0-8225-9721-7 (English edition, paperback)

LIBRARY OF CONGRESS
CATALOGING-IN-PUBLICATION DATA
Johnston, Joyce.
    Puerto Rico / by Joyce Johnston.
        p.   cm. — (Hello USA)
    Includes index.
    ISBN 0-8225-2752-9 (lib. bdg.)
    1. Puerto Rico—Juvenile literature.
    [1. Puerto Rico.] I. Title. II. Series.
F1958.3.J65   1994
972.95—dc20

93-36950
CIP
AC

Manufactured in the United States of America
2 3 4 5 6 – JR – 99 98 97 96 95

Cover photograph by Monica
Brown, Photographic Artist.

The glossary that begins on
page 68 gives definitions of
words shown in **bold type** in
the text.

 This book is printed
on acid-free, recycla-
ble paper.

CONTENTS

Scientists use the extra-large telescope at Arecibo Observatory to find and measure the giant gas clouds that move around in space.

Did You Know . . . ?

◼ The world's largest telescope is at Arecibo Observatory on Puerto Rico. The telescope's reflector was built to cover a huge natural sinkhole.

◼ The Milwaukee Deep off Puerto Rico's northern coast is one of the lowest places in the world. The underwater valley dips 28,000 feet (8,534 meters) below sea level.

◼ Northeastern Puerto Rico is home to a part of the Caribbean National Forest known as El Yunque. Besides Hawaii, El Yunque has the only **tropical rain forest** in the United States.

■ At Phosphorescent Bay, off the southeastern coast of Puerto Rico, millions of tiny organisms in the water give off a strange glow. The bay becomes a dazzling light show at night.

■ Puerto Rico's capital city—San Juan—was originally named Puerto Rico, and the island itself was called San Juan. Historians believe that the names were switched by mistake on an early map.

A Trip Around the Commonwealth

Millions of years ago, a chain of mountains southeast of Florida connected the eastern coast of North America with the northern coast of South America. Over time, the oceans rose and covered much of the land. Just the tops of these mountains still poke above the water, forming a string of islands about 2,000 miles (3,219 kilometers) long. The island chain, called the West Indies, stretches from Florida to Venezuela, in northern South America. Because they separate the Atlantic Ocean from the Caribbean Sea, the West Indies are sometimes called Caribbean islands.

Among these islands lies the Commonwealth of Puerto Rico. As a **commonwealth**, Puerto Rico governs itself but also belongs to the United States. The Puerto Ricans living on the island are U.S. citizens. They enjoy certain privileges, such as economic assistance and military protection from the United States.

Beautiful beaches and natural harbors have long attracted people to Puerto Rico's coasts. Puerto Rico means ''rich port'' in Spanish.

A quiet country inn lies on the island of Vieques.

Puerto Rico is made up of one large island and a number of smaller islands nearby. The large island is called Puerto Rico. Mona, Vieques, and Culebra are the largest of the other islands.

Puerto Rico's nearest neighbors are the Virgin Islands and the island of Hispaniola, which is shared by two countries—Haiti and the Dominican Republic. The Virgin Islands lie east of Puerto Rico across a strip of water called the Virgin Passage. Hispaniola is west of Puerto Rico across the Mona Passage.

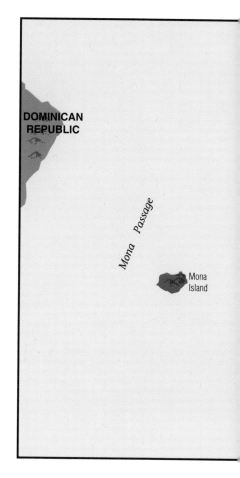

DOMINICAN
REPUBLIC

Mona Passage

Mona
Island

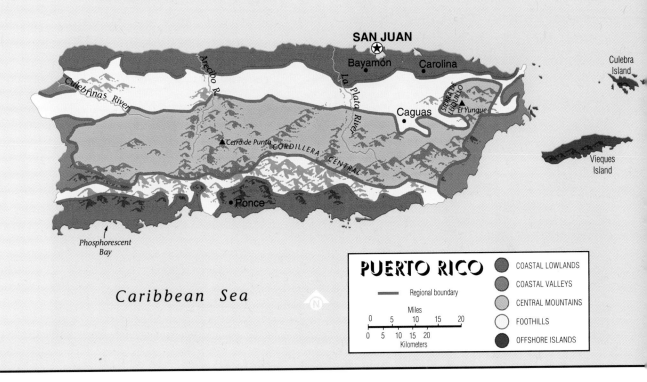

ATLANTIC OCEAN

SAN JUAN

Bayamón • Carolina

Culebra Island

Culebrinas River

Arecibo R.

La Plata River

SIERRA DE LUQUILLO

▲ El Yunque

Caguas

▲ Cerro de Punta

CORDILLERA CENTRAL

Vieques Island

• Ponce

↑ Phosphorescent Bay

Caribbean Sea

N

PUERTO RICO

Regional boundary

Miles
0   5   10   15   20

0 5 10 15 20
Kilometers

● COASTAL LOWLANDS

● COASTAL VALLEYS

○ CENTRAL MOUNTAINS

○ FOOTHILLS

● OFFSHORE ISLANDS

The main island of Puerto Rico has four land regions. They are the Coastal Lowlands, the Foothills, the Central Mountains, and the Coastal Valleys. The Coastal Lowlands—long, flat belts of land about 10 miles (16 km) wide—run along Puerto Rico's northern and southern coasts. Puerto Rico's largest cities are built on the Coastal Lowlands. Farms and sandy beaches are found on this part of the island, too.

The Foothills rise from the Coastal Lowlands toward the center of the island. At their lowest point, these hills rise only about 100 feet (30 m). Farther inland they reach 700 feet (213 m) in height.

The rugged peaks of the Central Mountains tower over the other land regions of Puerto Rico. A

Many palm trees grow on the Coastal Lowlands.

long, narrow mountain range—called the Cordillera Central—runs nearly the entire length of the island from west to east. Farmers grow coffee and fruit in the valleys between the steep mountain slopes. Cerro de Punta, the highest point on Puerto Rico, reaches 4,389 feet (1,338 m) in the Central Mountains. A small mountain range called Sierra de Luquillo rises in the eastern part of the region.

On the eastern and western coasts of Puerto Rico lie the Coastal Valleys. On a map, the valleys seem to poke into the mountains like fingers. Farmers grow sugarcane and coconuts and other fruits in these low, fertile areas.

Rising along the center of Puerto Rico, the peaks of the Cordillera Central form the backbone of the island.

The Fajardo River tumbles through the Foothills at the base of the Sierra de Luquillo.

Thousands of waterways spill down Puerto Rico's mountainsides. The island's rivers are short and shallow, so large boats cannot travel up or down them. Puerto Rico's major waterways include the Arecibo, La Plata, and Culebrinas rivers.

June through November is hurricane season in the West Indies. A hurricane, or severe tropical storm with strong winds and driving rains, lashes Puerto Rico about once every 10 years. In September 1989, Hurricane Hugo killed 12 Puerto Ricans and destroyed $1 billion worth of property on the island.

Most of the time, Puerto Rico's tropical weather is warm and calm. The average temperature in January is 73° F (23° C). In July it's a comfortable 80° F (27° C). Because the temperature almost never drops below 60° F (16° C), no snow falls on Puerto Rico—not even in the mountains.

Hurricane Hugo tore down thousands of trees and smashed many homes on Puerto Rico.

Rainfall is plentiful on the northern half of Puerto Rico, where about 70 inches (178 centimeters) of rain fall each year. As much as 200 inches (508 cm) drench the tropical rain forest of El Yunque each year. The southern part of the island is drier, receiving only about 37 inches (94 cm) of rain yearly.

15

Lush forests and wild plants once covered Puerto Rico. But by the mid-1900s, settlers had cut down most of the plants and trees to make room for farms. Only a few forests now dot the land. El Yunque is home to trees such as the palo colorado, the tabanuco, and the sierra palm.

Although the island has fewer forests than it once had, many types of trees and plants still grow there. The dry climate of southern Puerto Rico makes this area well suited for cactuses and bunch-grass. Palm trees, mangroves, and huge ceiba (silk-cotton) trees are just a few of the hundreds of kinds of trees that grow on the island. Hibiscus, poinsettias, and other colorful flowers also brighten the landscape.

One of Puerto Rico's smallest animals is the coquí. This tan-colored frog grows to only 1 inch (2.5 cm) in length and clings to damp leaves throughout the island. The coquí's two-note croak sounds like a bird's song. Other animals that live on Puerto Rico include snakes, iguanas, Puerto Rican parrots, and many other colorful birds that are found nowhere else in the United States.

Golden trumpets *(facing page)* **and other wildflowers dot the hills of Puerto Rico, where the tiny coquí** *(below)* **hops from leaf to leaf. Off Puerto Rico's coasts, colorful fish** *(right)* **look for food.**

Puerto Rico's Story

Shrieking parrots, thundering waves, and other wild noises of the forest and ocean were probably the only sounds on Puerto Rico 3,000 years ago. No human voices echoed through the island's valleys or drifted across its beaches.

No one is really sure when the first people landed on Puerto Rico. But at least 1,000 years ago, early inhabitants we now call American Indians canoed north from what is now Venezuela. Island by island, the Indians traveled farther until they explored and settled many Caribbean islands of the West Indies.

The first Indians to live on Puerto Rico were part of a group known as the Arawaks. They formed beautiful pots from clay and painted them red and white. The Arawaks made their homes on the island until around A.D. 600. Then they disappeared, although no one is sure why. Some experts believe that they died or ran away from war or disease.

By A.D. 1000, another group of people called the Taino were living on Puerto Rico and other islands of the West Indies. The Taino set up villages ruled by a *cacique,* or chief. The Indians built round houses by lining up the trunks of

The Taino lived in villages, where houses such as this one surrounded a central square.

palm trees in a circle, then topping them with cone-shaped roofs. At night the Taino slept in hammocks. During the day, they hunted, fished, and farmed.

At the town of Utuado, researchers have uncovered a Taino ballpark *(below),* used for a game in which players kept a ball in the air with any part of the body except the hands. Taino drawings *(right)* have also been discovered on rocks near the ballpark.

One of the Taino's most important crops was the yucca. The Indians ground the roots of this plant into flour for making bread called cassava. Taino farmers also grew corn, potatoes, beans, peanuts, peppers, cotton, and tobacco. For meat the Taino hunted iguanas and a small, furry animal called the hutia. Along the coasts, fishers gathered sea turtles, clams, snails, and a variety of fish to eat.

Each year the Taino took their crops to a storage center shared by the entire village.

The Taino called Puerto Rico Boriquen, which means "land of the brave lord" in their language. And Taino, their name for themselves, means "gentle." As the name suggests, the Taino were peaceful people.

But in the 1400s, this peace came to an end. The Taino's way of life was destroyed with the arrival of two new groups—the Carib Indians and the Spaniards. Like the Taino, the Caribs came to the West Indies from South America. They settled on nearby islands and frequently attacked the Taino—sometimes capturing Taino women and destroying villages.

The Caribs were skillful soldiers.

Christopher Columbus *(left)* claimed to have discovered every island he visited. He and his crew first tasted pineapple *(below)* on Puerto Rico or another nearby island.

Spain laid claim to Puerto Rico in 1493, when explorer Christopher Columbus landed on the island. Fifteen years later, Juan Ponce de León established a Spanish **colony,** or settlement, on Puerto Rico.

Spanish guards kept watch over Indians panning for gold in Puerto Rico's streams.

At first, the Taino welcomed the Spaniards. But the Spanish colonists forced the Taino—even children—to work long hours without pay. They dug for gold in Spanish mines on the island, planted and harvested the colonists' crops, and built their roads and houses.

The Taino wanted to get rid of the Spaniards but they had to be careful. They had never met people so different. And the colonists carried powerful weapons that were new to the Taino. Even so, the Indians began to think about fighting back.

Sinking Salcedo

Most of what we know about the Taino in the 1500s was written by Spaniards hundreds of years ago. Experts today believe that the stories may not be completely true.

Fact or fiction, this legend explains how Taino attacks on the Spanish soldiers first began. According to several Spanish history books, the Taino believed that the Spanish people —with their unusual clothes and powerful weapons—could not be killed. Having never seen a Spaniard die, the Taino decided to test this belief and came up with a plan.

A group of them agreed to guide a Spaniard named Diego Salcedo across the island. When Salcedo and the Indians came to a river, the Taino offered to carry the Spaniard across the water. Midway, the Indians dropped Salcedo and held him under the water for several hours.

For the next few days, they watched the body to make sure he was dead. Once the news spread that a Spanish person could be killed, the Taino began attacking the Spaniards, hoping to drive away the unwelcome intruders.

Although the Taino outnumbered the Spanish settlers, the Indians carried only stone axes into battle. The axes were useless against the Spaniards' powerful swords and guns. Ponce de León and his men killed hundreds of Taino, including Gueybaná, one of the most powerful Taino caciques.

After the battle, few Taino remained on Puerto Rico. Many had already died from Spanish diseases or from being overworked. Others joined their old enemies, the Caribs, who were fighting the Spaniards on nearby islands. But a few Taino stayed and married Spanish settlers.

Juan Ponce de León was the governor of Puerto Rico from 1509 to 1512.

Without the Taino to do their work, the Spaniards shipped people from Africa to Puerto Rico. The Spaniards forced the Africans to plant and harvest sugarcane, the colony's most important crop. Like the Taino before them, the African workers were slaves. By 1531 just

Slave traders went to Africa and loaded their ships with people to sell as slaves on Puerto Rico and on other islands of the West Indies.

To prevent captured Africans from fleeing, traders secured iron cuffs around the ankles, necks, or wrists of slaves en route to the Americas.

over 400 Spanish settlers and more than 2,000 African slaves were living on Puerto Rico.

The Spanish king allowed Puerto Rican settlers to trade only with Spain. This trade made the port city of San Juan an important stop for Spanish ships. But after Spain conquered other parts of America, Spanish ships did not stop very often on Puerto Rico. The traders could make more money from other colonies, which had more gold and silver.

But Puerto Rican colonists still needed food, clothes, tools, and other supplies to survive. So they illegally traded sugar, ginger, and other farm products in exchange for supplies from the French, British, and Dutch ships that anchored in Puerto Rico's ports.

The French, British, and Dutch wanted more from Puerto Rico than just sugar and ginger. They wanted some of the land that Columbus and other explorers had claimed for Spain. They also hoped to destroy Spain's power in the West Indies. In the 1500s and 1600s, France, Great Britain, and the Netherlands attacked Puerto Rico again and again.

To protect the port of San Juan, Spanish soldiers helped the colonists build a fortress overlooking San Juan Bay. Finished in 1540, the fortress was called La Fortaleza. Soon after, the Spaniards began building a second fort at San Juan named El Morro. Even with the new forts, Spain nearly lost Puerto Rico to the British and the

Spanish soldiers fired cannons from the forts of San Juan to defend Puerto Rico against enemy attacks.

For hundreds of years, El Morro was the strongest fort in the West Indies.

Dutch. But the Spaniards proved stronger, and by 1625 they had driven away the attackers.

Because Spain was a Catholic country, the Catholic church played an important part in the lives of Puerto Rico's colonists. Monks and nuns ran the churches, cared for the sick, and taught reading, writing, and religion to some of the colonists' children.

During the mid-1700s, Spain's leaders encouraged settlers to move to Puerto Rico by giving away free land. The colony's population began to grow rapidly. By 1765 nearly 45,000 people—including 5,037 slaves—lived in Puerto Rico's 24 towns. But the island still had only two schools. And because few roads led to outlying areas, only 5 percent of the land was being farmed. So the king of Spain ordered new schools and roads to be built, and San Juan's forts were strengthened.

31

By the late 1700s, Puerto Rico's population had grown to more than 150,000 people. Some of the new residents had arrived with the Spanish navy and stayed to live on the island. Others came to find work. Some newcomers were former slaves who had run away from nearby Caribbean islands owned by other European countries.

With a mixture of Spanish, Taino, and African roots, Puerto Rican culture was changing. Taino words had crept into the Spanish language used by Puerto Ricans. African traditions and Caribbean music were also part of the Puerto Rican way of life. And Puerto Rico had become wealthier than it had ever been before.

Many Puerto Ricans were unhappy with Spanish rule. They wanted more control over their lives than the king of Spain permitted. Merchants sought freedom to trade legally with other nations. Many people wanted to lower the taxes they paid to Spain. Most Puerto Ricans wanted

Many settlers in the late 1700s came to Puerto Rico to grow coffee. Coffee beans grow best at high elevations, so even longtime residents of the coasts moved to the mountains, hoping to get rich growing the crop.

the freedom to elect their own government officials. And they wished for better schools and hospitals and for more roads and bridges.

Around 1800, the countries of Spain, France, and Great Britain fought each other often. Because of these wars, the Spanish government did not have enough ships and soldiers to control its colonies. Spain began to allow Puerto Rico to trade with some other nations, including the United States. The Spanish king also granted Puerto Ricans several other freedoms.

In 1815 the king began to encourage people from other countries to settle in Puerto Rico. The new settlers, or **immigrants**, were given free land and did not have to pay taxes. This meant they could afford to plant vast fields of coffee beans, cotton, and cacao beans (for making chocolate) on **plantations,** or large farms.

Wealthy plantation owners in the 1800s had fancy homes with large gardens.

From 1820 to 1868, Rafael Cordero ran a free school in his home, where he taught any child who wanted to learn. Many of his students were the children of poor plantation workers and slaves.

The new plantation owners needed more and more slaves to work in their fields. By 1850 the number of African slaves on the island had risen to 51,000. On neighboring islands, such as the British West Indies and the French Antilles, slavery had been outlawed. Puerto Ricans who opposed slavery tried to persuade the Span-

Luis Muñoz Rivera

ish government to free Puerto Rico's slaves too. In 1868 Spain freed the children of Puerto Rican slaves. Spain ended slavery altogether in 1873, paying plantation owners for their loss of free laborers.

In the late 1800s, Spain still did not allow Puerto Ricans to elect their own government officials. But in 1897, Puerto Rico finally won the right to vote. The next year, they elected Luis Muñoz Rivera to lead the new government.

Just as the new government took office, Spain clashed with the United States and the Spanish-American War began. Within a few months, U.S. forces landed on the southern coast of Puerto Rico. On December 10, 1898, Spain surrendered Puerto Rico to the United States.

The U.S. military marched through San Juan after taking over Puerto Rico.

The United States gave Puerto Ricans even less freedom than Spain had given them. At first the U.S. military occupied the island and ran the Puerto Rican government. But by 1917, Puerto Ricans became U.S. citizens. That same year, the United States began allowing the people of Puerto Rico to elect some of their government officials.

But U.S. companies controlled much of the island's economy. For example, American businesses owned most of the island's sugar plantations and the mills that made the cane into sugar. The companies paid very low wages to

Puerto Rican workers. The sugar was sent to the U.S. mainland, where it was sold for huge profits—which benefited the companies but not the island's workers. Puerto Ricans earned so little money that by the 1920s, Puerto Rico was known as the Poorhouse of the Caribbean.

In the early 1900s, many Puerto Ricans lived in dirty, crowded neighborhoods.

To improve the economy, the Puerto Rican government began a program in 1947 called Operation Bootstrap. Through this program, the government supplied more electricity so new factories could be opened. Operation Bootstrap offered loans to businesses and encouraged foreign companies to move to Puerto Rico, creating more jobs for Puerto Ricans. Because of Operation Bootstrap, business grew and Puerto Ricans made more money.

At the same time, the U.S. government permitted Puerto Ricans to choose their own governor. In 1948 Luis Muñoz Marín, the son of Muñoz Rivera, was elected to the post. Muñoz Marín and several

In the late 1940s, Puerto Rican workers found jobs in paper plants and other factories.

groups in Puerto Rico worked to reshape Puerto Rico's relationship with the United States. They also wrote a **constitution,** or set of laws, for Puerto Rico.

On July 1, 1952, the U.S. government approved the constitution for Puerto Rico. On July 25, Puerto Rico became the Commonwealth of Puerto Rico. But the new constitution and official name did not permanently settle questions about the future of the island.

Since the 1950s, Puerto Ricans have disagreed over what is best for the island. Some Puerto Ricans have wanted their island to become a nation independent of the United States. Others have argued that Puerto Rico should remain a commonwealth. Still others have favored making Puerto Rico a U.S. state.

Puerto Rico's Choices

As a state:
Puerto Ricans...

★ would vote for U.S. president.

★ would pay U.S. federal taxes.

★ would probably study Spanish and English in school.

As a commonwealth:
Puerto Ricans...

★ do not vote for U.S. president.

★ do not pay U.S. federal taxes.

★ study mainly Spanish in school.

As an independent nation:
Puerto Ricans...

★ would elect their own president.

★ would pay their own federal taxes.

★ would continue studying mainly Spanish in school.

A.D. 1000   1493   1540   1818   1873

Taino Indians build
villages on what is
now Puerto Rico

Columbus claims Puerto
Rico for Spain

Workers finish La Fortaleza and
begin building El Morro

Spanish king awards free land to
new settlers

Slavery is outlawed on
Puerto Rico

In November 1993, Puerto Ricans voted on which of the three options they preferred. With most voters participating, Puerto Rico supported the commonwealth choice over the options of statehood or independence. As a commonwealth, Puerto Rico hopes to keep its ties to the United States, while preserving a strong sense of Puerto Rican culture. And Puerto Ricans will continue to think about the best ways to improve life on their island.

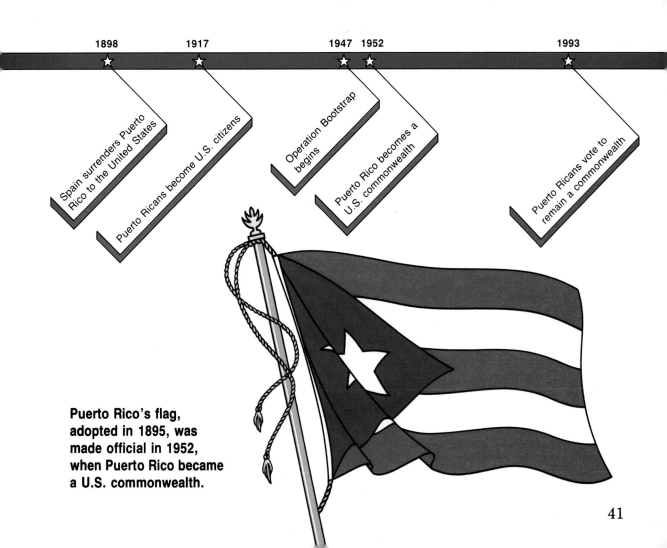

1898 — Spain surrenders Puerto Rico to the United States

1917 — Puerto Ricans become U.S. citizens

1947 — Operation Bootstrap begins

1952 — Puerto Rico becomes a U.S. commonwealth

1993 — Puerto Ricans vote to remain a commonwealth

Puerto Rico's flag, adopted in 1895, was made official in 1952, when Puerto Rico became a U.S. commonwealth.

Living and Working on Puerto Rico

For a long time, sugarcane, tobacco, coffee beans, and ginger were the mainstays of Puerto Rico's economy. But since Operation Bootstrap brought factories to Puerto Rico in the mid-1900s, manufacturing has become the island's most important industry.

Almost one out of every five Puerto Rican workers is employed

A student *(opposite page)* **passes by a mural in Dorado, Puerto Rico. A lab worker** *(right)* **sorts through thousands of pills before the medication is bottled.**

in the island's 2,000 factories. Some factory workers package medicines or assemble machinery or scientific instruments. Others sew clothes and leather goods, such as gloves and shoes. Still others make copper wire, television sets, rum, and cameras. At Puerto Rico's sugar mills, the island's sugarcane is processed into sugar.

43

One in five farmers in Puerto Rico grows sugarcane *(left)*. Bananas *(below)* are the island's most important fruit crop.

Farms cover one-third of the land on Puerto Rico. But only 4 percent of Puerto Ricans farm the land, and the value of the island's crops is small. Some farms produce milk, poultry, and eggs. Many farmers raise cattle for beef. In

44

addition to sugar, coffee, and tobacco, fruits—such as bananas, pineapples, and coconuts—are grown on Puerto Rico.

Some Puerto Ricans earn their living from the ocean waters. Fishers catch about 4.5 million pounds (2 million kilograms) of fish every year. Lobster and tuna are Puerto Rico's most valuable catches.

A man selling fish in San Juan shows off the catch of the day.

The government employs the largest number of Puerto Ricans. People working for the Puerto Rican government run government offices, teach in schools, and care for the sick in hospitals. U.S. government workers on Puerto Rico serve in the military or protect wildlife in the Caribbean National Forest. Both the U.S. Navy and the U.S. Army have military bases on Puerto Rican land.

The government is just one of many service industries on Puerto Rico. Other service workers sell goods or help people and businesses on the island. Clothing, medicines, and sugar are the most important goods that service workers buy and sell in Puerto Rico.

A teacher looks over her lesson plans.

46

Many of Puerto Rico's service workers have jobs in tourism. Restaurant cooks, tour guides, hotel managers, and travel agents help the island's visitors enjoy their vacations. About 2.5 million tourists from the U.S. mainland and from around the world visit Puerto Rico every year.

When tourists visit, they rub elbows with Puerto Rico's 3.2 million residents. Puerto Rico's large population squeezes into an area smaller than the state of Connecticut, making the island more crowded than any of the 50 states. Two out of every three Puerto Ricans live in the island's cities.

Many workers in San Juan have jobs in the city's bustling financial district.

Millions More on the Mainland

Puerto Rico has a large population, but in addition to the islanders, another 2.7 million Puerto Ricans live on the U.S. mainland. About half of these Puerto Ricans live in the New York City area. With such a large number of Puerto Ricans and other Latinos (people from Latin America), New York has several Spanish-language newspapers, radio programs, and television shows. The part of the city where many Puerto Ricans live—East Harlem—is known as *el barrio,* which means "the neighborhood" in Spanish.

San Juan is Puerto Rico's capital and largest city. Long ago, the city spread beyond the walls the Spaniards had built to enclose it. The area surrounding San Juan includes the island's second largest city, Bayamón. Ponce, the third largest city, lies near the middle of the southern coast. Other large cities include Caguas and Carolina.

The ancestors of most Puerto Ricans were Spanish, African, and American Indian. But people from many other places have also settled on Puerto Rico. Some Puerto Ricans can trace their ancestry to

Denmark, France, Great Britain, Germany, the United States, or Cuba. The island's ethnic mixture colors every part of Puerto Rican life, from music and art to religion and education.

Fiestas, or festivals, are an important part of life on Puerto Rico. Every year each town on the island hosts its own religious fiesta, complete with parades, parties, and ceremonies. The Festival of San Juan, celebrated yearly on June 24, includes carnivals, dances, and music for several days before and after the holiday.

Musicians from around the world travel to Puerto Rico each year to play music at the Casals Festival. The festival, held in San Juan, is named in honor of Pablo Casals, a famous cellist who lived on Puerto Rico.

Each year on January 6, Puerto Ricans celebrate Three Kings' Day—a traditional Spanish holiday—with a fiesta.

In San Juan, sunbathers looking across the bay can see huge modern hotels next to a timeworn fort.

Visitors to San Juan can walk the narrow streets of Old San Juan, the section of the city that is still partially surrounded by walls. People also can visit the Church of San José, which was built in 1532. Or they can explore El Morro, the fort where Spaniards hid from enemy armies hundreds of years ago.

Art and music lovers will find many things to do on Puerto Rico. In the city of San Germán is a church called Porta Coeli (Gates of Heaven). Built in 1606, the church now exhibits religious art. The Ponce Museum of Art displays the works of Puerto Rican and European artists. Plays, operas,

Visitors to Old San Juan enjoy the area's narrow brick roads and colorful old buildings.

and concerts are performed at the Centro de Bellas Artes in San Juan.

Cockfighting is one of the most popular sports on Puerto Rico. In a cockfight, two cocks, or male chickens, attack each other. Many sports fans also enjoy the horse races at El Nuevo Comandante Racetrack.

Baseball, basketball, and boxing are also popular. Islanders enjoy baseball year-round, since their ball season begins just as the U.S. mainland season ends. Some famous major-league players, such as Toronto Blue Jay Roberto Alomar and former Pittsburgh Pirate Roberto Clemente, began their careers on Puerto Rico.

Many tourists visit Puerto Rico for the beaches and the warm, blue seawater surrounding the island. Deep-sea fishing, scuba diving, and swimming are popular activities year-round.

Off the island of Culebra, underwater snorklers discover colorful tropical fish darting through reefs of coral. Boaters and swimmers might spot a leatherback sea turtle, which can grow almost seven feet (2 m) long. Hikers can explore El Yunque in search of the rare Puerto Rican parrot.

Puerto Rico offers plenty of adventure underground, too. In

A scuba diver greets a lobster.

Río Camuy Cave Park, located on northwestern Puerto Rico, tourists can hike along one of the largest underground rivers in the world. On Mona Island, visitors can explore caves that were once home to pirates. Perhaps a pirate even left a buried treasure behind!

Underwater explorers may discover sunken ships (right) **off Puerto Rico's coasts. Rock formations** (far right) **that look like icicles hang from the ceiling of a cave in Río Camuy Cave Park.**

Protecting the Environment

Puerto Rican parrots are hard to find. Their feathers are green, like the leaves of the trees in El Yunque—the rain forest where the birds live. The red spots on the birds' foreheads and the blue patches on their wings help a careful bird-watcher see the parrots. But the parrots are hard to find not only because they blend in so well with their surroundings but also because there are so few of them.

Christopher Columbus probably saw a lot of Puerto Rican parrots when he landed on Puerto Rico in 1493. Scientists think that as many as one million Puerto Rican parrots lived on the island at that time. But nowadays only about 100 exist. By learning how the parrots nest and raise their young, people can better understand what has happened to the birds since the Spaniards first settled on the island.

A pair of Puerto Rican parrots peek out from their nest.

After a parrot chooses its mate, they both look for a big old tree in which to build their nest. They need a tree with a dry cavity, or hole between 23 and 50 feet (7 and 15 m) above the ground. In the nest, the female parrot lays two to four eggs. She then sits on her eggs for about one month. When the young parrots peck their way out of the eggs, they are nearly featherless. But within nine weeks, the young birds have grown enough feathers to fly.

When Columbus landed on Puerto Rico, forests covered most of the island. Parrots could find plenty of large trees with cavities big enough for nests. But by 1912, as much as 80 percent of the forests on Puerto Rico had been cut down to make room for farms, towns, and cities.

This **deforestation,** or clearing of forests, left the parrots with far fewer nesting trees. Parrots that could not find nesting places did not lay eggs. As a result, fewer baby parrots were born, and the parrot population dwindled. By 1940 Puerto Rican parrots could be found only in El Yunque.

A bird's-eye view of the island shows how much of the land is used for farming *(above)* **and cities** *(left).*

Although the trees in El Yunque are big enough for parrot nests, the forest is much wetter than the forests in which the Puerto Rican parrots originally lived. Some of the cavities fill with water, making it impossible for the parrots to build nests in them.

Conditions can worsen in the summer and fall, when hurricanes threaten. These powerful storms rip through the forest, destroying nests and injuring or killing the birds.

Parrots also have had to compete with birds called thrashers and with bees from nearby farms. The thrashers and the bees also

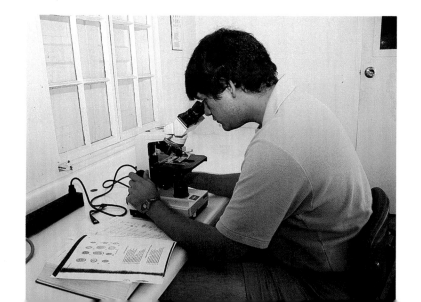

A scientist in El Yunque studies parasites—tiny organisms that are harmful to the parrots.

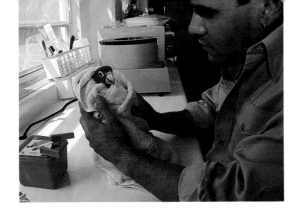

Scientists care for baby parrots *(left)* and set up artificial nesting cavities *(below)* in the forest.

use tree cavities. By 1975 only 13 parrots were found living in El Yunque.

Since then scientists have been working to increase the number of parrots on Puerto Rico. Researchers have built artificial nesting cavities for the parrots to use. They have also built boxes for thrashers to nest in, leaving more natural cavities for parrot nests. Workers keep nesting places dry and clean and watch over the new parrot chicks to make sure they are safe and healthy.

59

Sick or injured parrots sometimes are taken from the wild and put in an aviary, where the birds are cared for until they heal.

Workers have also placed some parrot eggs in **incubators,** or heated containers that keep the eggs warm enough to hatch. Once the baby birds leave their shells and become strong, they live in protected **aviaries,** or large bird cages. Some of these parrots grow to adulthood and raise their young in the aviaries. Other birds are set free in El Yunque, where the parrot population has increased to more than 40.

In the future, scientists plan to release some of the parrots in other forests on Puerto Rico. As these birds raise their young in their new homes, the wild parrot population will continue to grow. Puerto Ricans hope that these efforts to save the Puerto Rican parrot will succeed.

A painting on a school wall reminds students of the Puerto Rican parrot's beauty and importance.

Puerto Rico's Famous People

ACTORS & ENTERTAINERS

José Ferrer (1912–1992), the star of many films and stage productions, was born in Santurce, Puerto Rico. In 1950 he won an Academy Award for his role in *Cyrano de Bergerac*. Ferrer became a member of the Theater Hall of Fame in 1981.

Raúl Juliá (1940–1994) was an actor from San Juan. His many roles included Count Dracula in a Broadway production and Rafael the Fixit Man on television's "Sesame Street." Julia also starred in the films *Presumed Innocent* and *The Addams Family*.

Rita Moreno (born 1931) is an actress, dancer, and singer from Humacao, Puerto Rico. She is probably best known for her role as Anita in *West Side Story*. Moreno is the only woman ever to win all four of the entertainment world's highest awards— she has an Oscar, a Grammy, a Tony, and two Emmys.

◀ JOSÉ FERRER

▲ RAÚL JULIÁ

◀ RITA MORENO

▼ FRANCISCO OLLER

ROBERTO ALOMAR ▲

ARTIST

Francisco Oller y Cestero (1833–1917), one of Puerto Rico's most famous artists, completed more than 800 paintings during his long life. Many of Oller's works portray his antislavery views. The artist from Bayamón also painted Puerto Rican landscapes.

ATHLETES

Roberto Alomar (born 1968) is a baseball player from Ponce. Playing second base with the Toronto Blue Jays, he won the Golden Glove Award in 1992 and helped the team win the World Series in 1993.

Roberto Walker Clemente (1934–1972), of Carolina, Puerto Rico, was one of baseball's greatest players. As an outfielder for the Pittsburgh Pirates, he earned the Golden Glove Award 12 times. Clemente died in a plane crash. Soon after, he was elected to the National Baseball Hall of Fame.

Gigi Fernández (born 1964), a world-class tennis player from San Juan, was named the Puerto Rican Female Athlete of the Year in 1988. She won U.S. Open doubles championships in 1988, 1990, and 1992. In 1992 Fernández and her partner won Olympic gold medals in doubles tennis.

Juan ("Chi Chi") Rodríguez (born 1934), from Río Piedras, Puerto Rico, became a professional golfer in 1960. Since then, Rodríguez has been one of the most popular and talented golfers in the United States.

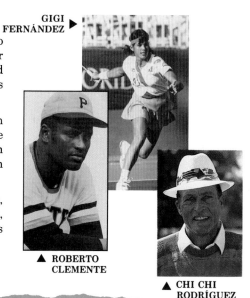

◀ GIGI FERNÁNDEZ

▲ ROBERTO CLEMENTE

▲ CHI CHI RODRÍGUEZ

◀ JOSÉ FELICIANO

▼ PABLO CASALS

MUSICIANS

Pablo Casals (1876–1973) was a world-famous cellist, composer, and conductor who moved from Spain to Puerto Rico in 1956. Casals founded the Puerto Rico Symphony Orchestra and began the Casals Festival—a yearly musical event in San Juan that attracts musicians and music lovers from around the world.

José Feliciano (born 1945) moved from Lares, Puerto Rico, to New York City, where he began his musical career in the early 1960s. Born blind, he taught himself to sing and to play many musical instruments. In 1968 Feliciano won Grammy Awards for best male pop singer and for best new artist. Many people know his popular Christmas song, "Feliz Navidad."

POLITICIANS

Herman Badillo (born 1929), from Caguas, Puerto Rico, moved to New York City in 1941. He became the first Puerto Rican to be elected to the U.S. Congress, where he served from 1971 to 1977. Badillo has headed the Governor's Advisory Committee on Hispanic Affairs in New York since 1983.

Luis Muñoz Marín (1898–1980), born in San Juan, was the first elected governor of Puerto Rico, serving from 1948 to 1964. Muñoz Marín helped develop Operation Bootstrap, a plan to spur Puerto Rico's economy. He also set up Puerto Rico's commonwealth relationship with the United States.

◀ HERMAN BADILLO

▲ LUIS MUÑOZ MARÍN

LUIS MUÑOZ RIVERA ▶

▲ FELISA RINCÓN DE GAUTIER

RAMÓN EMETERIO ▶ BETANCES

Luis Muñoz Rivera (1859–1916), the father of Muñoz Marín, was a newspaper editor and politician from Barranquitas, Puerto Rico. He worked with Spanish officials and later with the U.S. government to gain more rights for Puerto Ricans.

Felisa Rincón de Gautier (1897–1994) was born in San Juan, where she served as mayor from 1946 to 1968. Named Woman of the Year in the Americas in 1954, she presided over the Inter-American Organization of Municipalities the same year.

SOCIAL LEADERS

Ramón Emeterio Betances (1827–1898) was a doctor and social reformer who worked to rid Puerto Rico of diseases such as cholera and led the fight to outlaw slavery. Betances was from Cabo Rojo, Puerto Rico.

Antonia Coello Novello (born 1944) from Fajardo, Puerto Rico, is a well-known leader and researcher in the field of children's health. In 1989 she became the first person of Latino roots to be named U.S. surgeon general.

Arthur Schomburg (1874–1938), from San Juan, moved in 1891 to New York, where he led black cultural groups and began a collection of documents from African American history. The collection, which Schomburg later oversaw at the New York Public Library, was named after him upon his death.

▲ ARTHUR
SCHOMBURG

◄ RENÉ
MARQUES

▲ CONCHA
MELÉNDEZ

▲ LOLA RODRIGUEZ
DE TÍO

WRITERS

Eugenio María de Hostos (1839–1903), born in Río Cañas, Puerto Rico, wrote a variety of books including children's stories and the novel *La Peregrinación de Bayoán*. Hostos also fought to provide a free education for all Puerto Rican children.

René Marqués (1919–1979) was a playwright and short-story author from Arecibo, Puerto Rico. His most famous play—*La Carreta*—was first seen in 1953 and was published in 1961. The play came out in English as *The Oxcart* in 1969.

Concha Meléndez (1892–1990) was a well-known poet. She also wrote many books and essays about the works of famous writers from different Latin American countries. Meléndez was born in Caguas, Puerto Rico.

Lola Rodriguez de Tío (1854–1924), from San Germán, wrote poetry and songs, including the Puerto Rican anthem, "La Borinqueña." Her longest work, *Mis Cantares,* is a collection of 2,500 poems.

Facts-at-a-Glance

Nickname: *Isla del Encanto*
  (Island of Enchantment)
Song: "La Borinqueña"
Motto: *Joannes est nomen ejus*
  (John Is His Name)
Flower: maga
Tree: ceiba (kapok)
Bird: reinita

Population: 3,522,037*
Area: 3,515 sq mi (9,104 sq km)
Became a commonwealth: July 25, 1952
Capital: San Juan
Major cities (and populations*):
  San Juan (437,745), Bayamón (220,262),
  Ponce (187,749), Carolina (177,806),
  Caguas (133,447)
U.S. representatives: 1, nonvoting

Places to visit: Caguana Indian Ceremonial Park near Utuado, Phosphorescent Bay near La Parguera, Torrecilla Baja near Loíza, San Juan Museum of Arts and History in Old San Juan, Sun Bay on Vieques, El Yunque rain forest in the Caribbean National Forest

Annual events: Carnaval in Ponce (Feb.), Dulce Sueño Paso Fino Horse Show in Guayama (Feb.), Casals Festival in San Juan (June), Fiesta de Santiago Apostol in Loíza (July), Indian Festival in Jayuya (Nov.)

*1990 census

Natural resources: warm and moist climate, rivers, salt, sand, soil, clay, gravel, stone

Agricultural products: sugarcane, coffee, bananas, plantains, pineapples, cattle, poultry, eggs, honey, avocados, coconuts, citrus fruits

Manufactured goods: medicines, machinery, food products, clothing, electronics equipment, leather products, stone, clay, and glass products

ENDANGERED SPECIES

Mammals—West Indian manatee, fin whale, humpback whale, Sei whale, sperm whale

Birds—Puerto Rican parrot, brown pelican, peregrine falcon, yellow-shouldered blackbird, Puerto Rican nightjar

Reptiles—Puerto Rican boa, leatherback sea turtle, hawksbill sea turtle, Culebra giant anole

Plants—Vahl's boxwood, elfin tree fern, beautiful goetzea, Wheeler's peperomia, palo colorado

WHERE PUERTO RICANS WORK
Services—49 percent
   (Services includes jobs in trade; community, social
   & personal services; finance, insurance, & real es-
   tate; transportation, communication, & utilities)
Manufacturing—18 percent
Government—23 percent
Construction—6 percent
Agriculture—4 percent

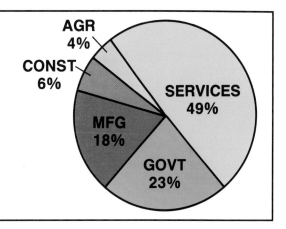

AGR 4%
CONST 6%
MFG 18%
SERVICES 49%
GOVT 23%

PRONUNCIATION GUIDE

Arecibo (ah-ray-SEE-boh)

Bayamón (bah-yah-MOHN)

Caguas (KAH-gwahs)

Cordillera Central
(kor-dee-YEH-rah sen-TRAHL)

Culebra (koo-LAY-brah)

El Yunque (el YOON-kay)

Muñoz Marín, Luis
(MOON-yohs mah-REEN, loo-EES)

Ponce de León, Juan
(POHN-say day lay-OHN, HWAHN)

San Juan (SAHN HWAHN)

Sierra de Luquillo
(see-EHR-rah day loo-KEE-yoh)

Taino (TAY-noh)

Vieques (vee-AY-kehs)

Glossary

aviary A large cage or building for keeping wild birds in captivity.

colony A territory ruled by a country some distance away.

commonwealth A territory (or other political unit) that has power over its own local affairs but that is voluntarily tied to a larger nation through shared laws and rights. The Puerto Rican term for commonwealth, *estado libre asociado,* means associated free state.

constitution The system of basic laws or rules of a government, society, or organization. The document in which these laws or rules are written.

deforestation The large-scale cutting or burning of trees and other plants in a forest.

immigrant A person who moves into a foreign land and settles there.

incubator A container equipped with heat and lights to keep bird eggs warm enough to hatch.

plantation A large estate, usually in a warm climate, on which crops are grown by workers who live on the estate. In the past, plantation owners usually used slave labor.

tropical rain forest A thick, wet, evergreen forest with an annual rainfall of more than 100 inches (254 cm). Tropical rain forests are located in hot, wet climates near the equator.

Index

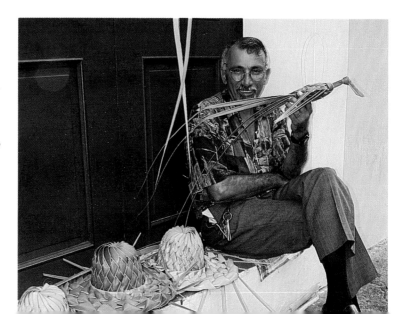

Acknowledgments:

Maryland Cartographics, pp. 2, 10–11; NE Stock Photos: © Joseph V. Hollweg, pp. 2–3, © Margo Taussig Pinkerton, p. 10, © Jim Schwabel, p. 57 (right); Puerto Rico Federal Affairs Administration, pp. 6, 21 (left); Jack Lindstrom, p. 7; Marvin W. Schwartz, pp. 9, 43, 47; © Thomas R. Fletcher, pp. 12, 13, 14, 15, 16, 17 (left), 18–19, 30, 31, 44 (right), 49, 51, 55, 69; JAIME LAUREANO / AQUA GRAPHICS / CHICAGO, pp. 17 (right), 52, 53 (left & right); Puerto Rico General Archives, pp. 20, 25, 26, 28, 29, 33, 35, 37, 38, 62 (bottom right), 64 (bottom left & bottom center), 65 (bottom left, right, & center); Leslie Fagre, p. 21 (right); Independent Picture Service, p. 22; Bodleian Library, University of Oxford, p. 23; Knights of Columbus Headquarters Museum, p. 24 (left); James Ford Bell Library, University of Minnesota, p. 24 (right); *Dictionary of American Portraits*, p. 27; Department of Agriculture of Puerto Rico, p. 32; Archives of the Audio-Visual Unit / Art Museum of the Americas / OAS, p. 34; National Archives, Neg. no. 126-PG-5G-9, p. 36; © W. Lynn Seldon, Jr., pp. 42, 71; Eugene G. Schulz, pp. 44 (left), 45, 46, 50, 57 (left); © Richard B. Levine, p. 48; U.S. Fish and Wildlife Service: Tomás Carlo, p. 55 (inset), José Colón, p. 56, Jafet Vélez, pp. 58, 59 (left & right), 61, Luther C. Goldman, p. 60; Hollywood Book & Poster Co., p. 62 (top left & top right); Kenneth G. Lawrence's Movie Memorabilia Shop of Hollywood, p. 62 (top center); Toronto Blue Jays Baseball Club, p. 62 (bottom left); Pittsburgh Pirates, p. 63 (top left); Carol Newsom, p. 63 (top center); Headshot Archives / © PGA Tour, p. 63 (top right); RCA Records, p. 63 (bottom left); Festival Casals, p. 63 (bottom right); Herman Badillo, p. 64 (top left); Commonwealth of Puerto Rico, Department of State, p. 64 (top right & bottom right); Moorland-Spingarn Research Center, Howard University, p. 65 (top left); Office of the U.S. surgeon general, p. 65 (top right); Jean Matheny, p. 66.